T0405561

FARMER LLAMA'S FARM MACHINES

PLOWS

BY KIRSTY HOLMES

BEARPORT
PUBLISHING

Minneapolis, Minnesota

Library of Congress Cataloging-in-Publication Data is available at www.loc.gov or upon request from the publisher.

ISBN: 978-1-64747-544-4 (hardcover)
ISBN: 978-1-64747-551-2 (paperback)
ISBN: 978-1-64747-558-1 (ebook)

For more information, write to Bearport Publishing, 5357 Penn Avenue South, Minneapolis, MN 55419. Printed in the United States of America.

IMAGE CREDITS

All images are courtesy of Shutterstock.com, unless otherwise specified. With thanks to Getty Images, Thinkstock Photo, and iStockphoto. Cover - NotionPic, Tartila, A-R-T, logika600, BiterBig, Hennadii. Aggie - NotionPic, Tartila. Grid - BiterBig. Farm - Faber14. Spreaders - Hennadii H. 2 - alazur. 4 - Mascha Tace. 6-7 - Hennadii H, K-Nick. 8 - Nsit, firtinali. 9 - Magicleaf. 10 - judyjump, Hennadii H. 12 - Katason. 13 - panotthorn phuhual, ananaline, NotionPic, KC Melete. 14 - Anest, studioworkstock. 15 - Hennadii H. 16 - Scharfsinn. 17 - Rachael Arnott. 19 - BigMouse, Conny Sjostrom. 21 - ArtMalivanov, DRogatnev. 22 - AVIcon, alexandrovskyi, Olha Bocharova. 23 - shaineast.

CONTENTS

Down on the Farm! 4

What Is a Plow? 6

The History of Plows 8

Types of Plows 12

A Job for a Plow 14

Plowing around the World............. 16

Record Breakers..................... 18

Get Your Llama-Diploma 20

Asleep on the Job 22

Glossary 24

Index................................ 24

DOWN ON THE FARM!

Welcome! My name is Aggie. I'm a farmer llama here at Happy Valley Farm. You must be the new **farmhand**.

It's spring, so it's time to get the soil ready for the new seeds. Let's get you trained in!

What You Need to Know

What are the oxen for? ☐

What does soil need? ☐

What do plows do? ☐

How do plows work? ☐

WHAT IS A PLOW?

A plow is a tool that turns over the soil in a field. The plow is usually connected to a tractor, which pulls it along.

SOIL

Soil must be turned over at the end of winter. This **buries** any bits of old **crops** in the ground. Turning also digs out **weeds** and makes the soil loose.

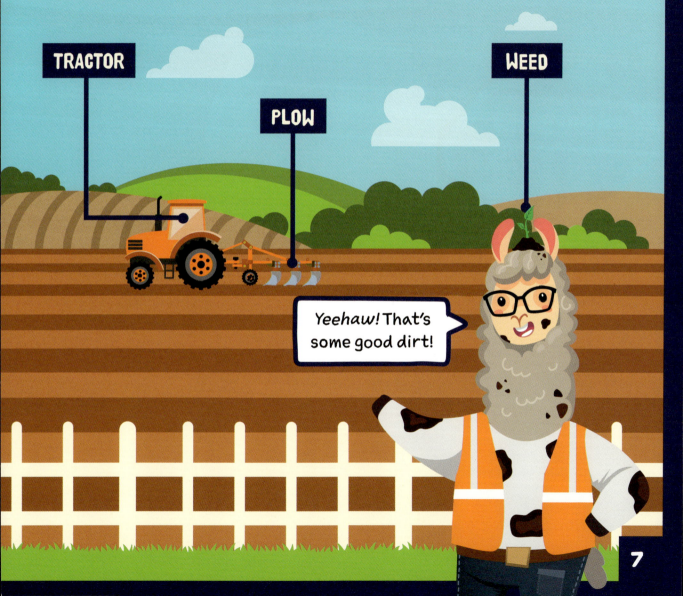

TRACTOR

PLOW

WEED

Yeehaw! That's some good dirt!

THE HISTORY OF PLOWS

Since people started farming, farmers have turned soil. Turning the soil is also called tilling or cultivating. Let's look at how it all began . . .

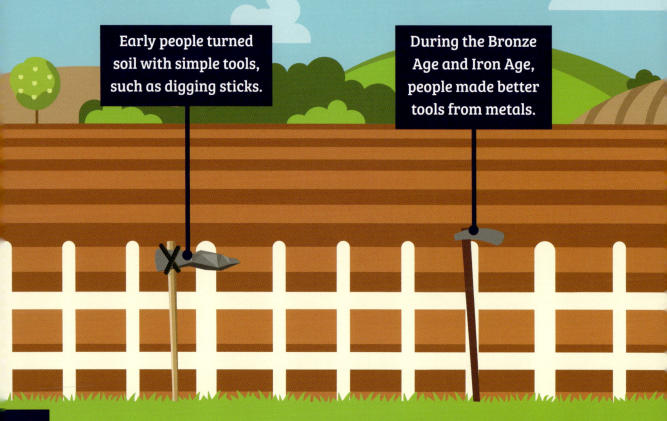

Early people turned soil with simple tools, such as digging sticks.

During the Bronze Age and Iron Age, people made better tools from metals.

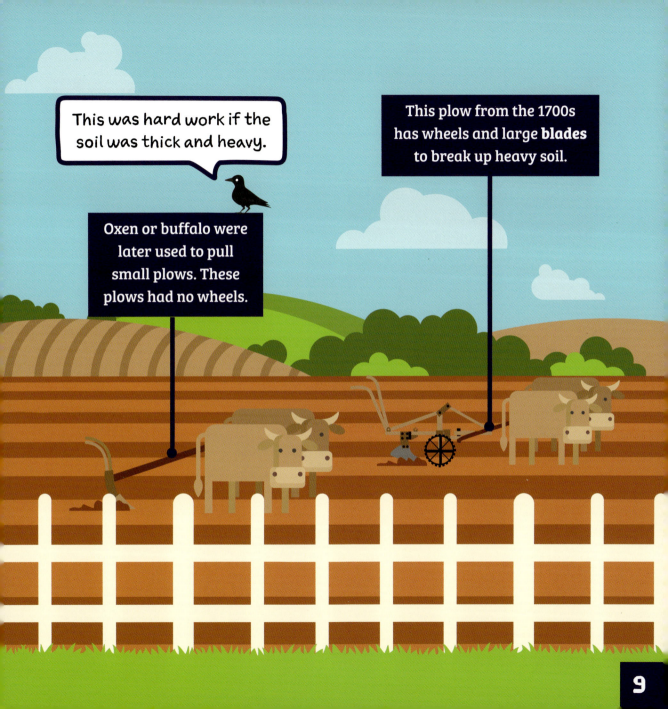

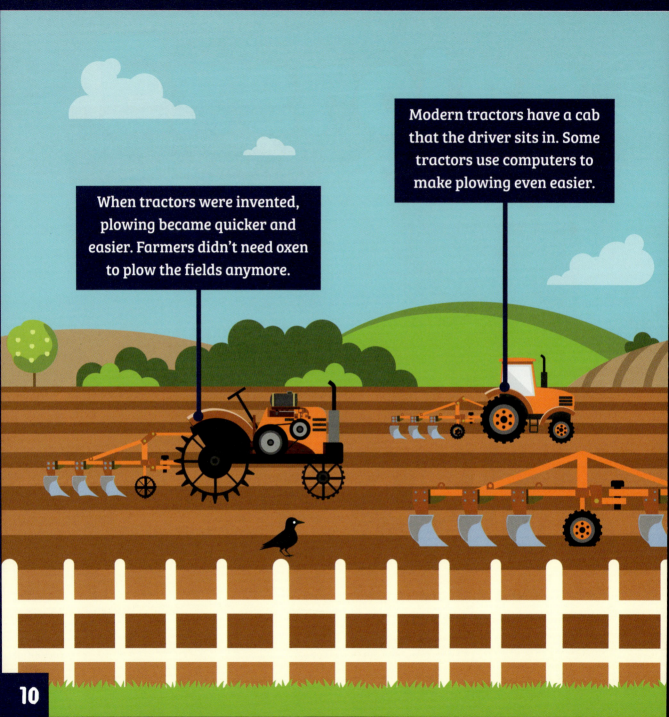

When tractors were invented, plowing became quicker and easier. Farmers didn't need oxen to plow the fields anymore.

Modern tractors have a cab that the driver sits in. Some tractors use computers to make plowing even easier.

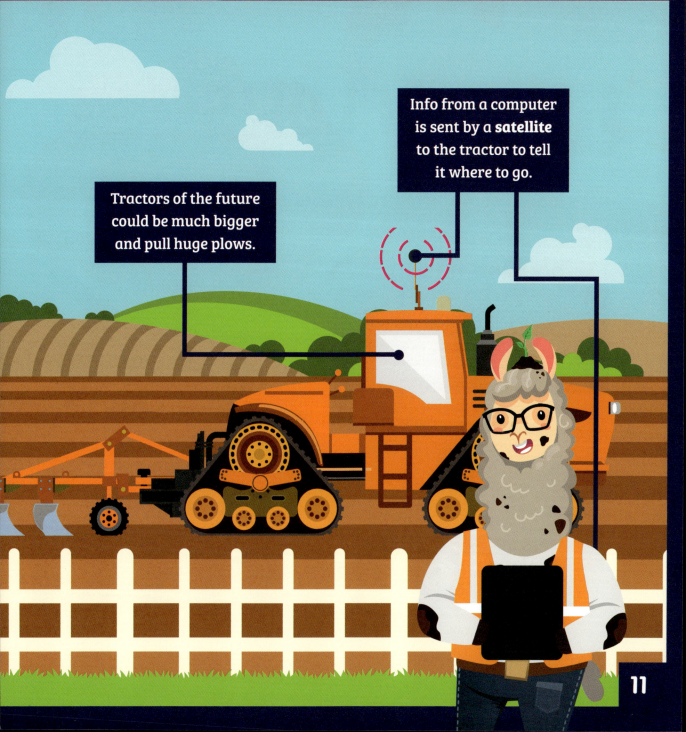

Tractors of the future could be much bigger and pull huge plows.

Info from a computer is sent by a **satellite** to the tractor to tell it where to go.

TYPES OF PLOWS

Let's look at some different types of plows.

MOLDBOARD PLOW

Moldboard plows have large, curved blades that cut the soil. The soil is pushed upward and turned over as the tractor pulls the plow along.

MOLDBOARD

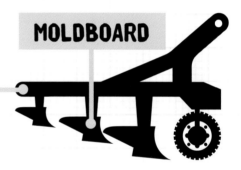

CHISEL PLOW

Chisel plows are also called rippers — and for good reason! They have sharp, pointed shovels.

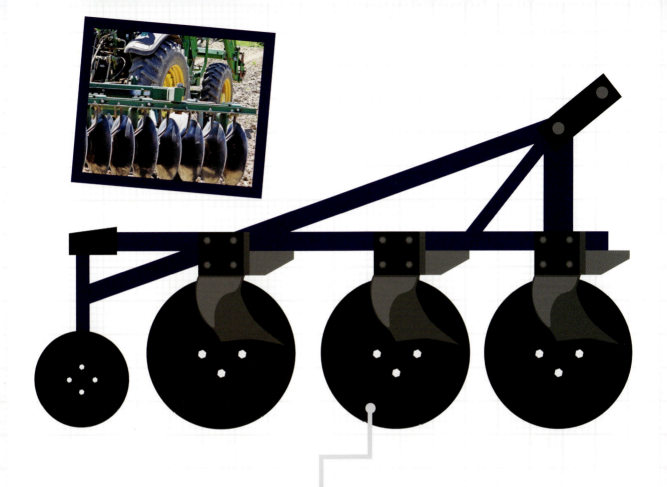

DISC PLOW

Disc plows have round, flat discs instead of blades.
They are really good for turning hard soil.

A JOB FOR A PLOW

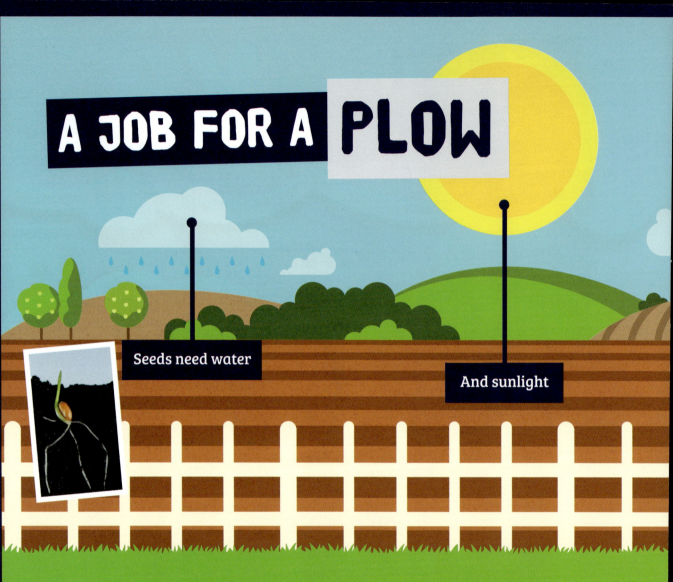

Seeds need water

And sunlight

Farmers bury different seeds at different **depths**. This makes sure the seeds get the right amount of the things they need.

If the soil is too hard or flat, air, water, and sunlight can't get to the seeds. The plow stirs up the soil. This adds air to the soil and lets the water and sunlight through.

And soil

Seeds need sunlight, water, and soil. They also need the perfect temperature.

Looks like seed success!

PLOWING AROUND
THE WORLD

The plow is used all around the world. It is an important tool in growing all sorts of crops.

WATER BUFFALO

CHINA

Rice is grown in paddy fields in China. Water buffalo can be used to plow these wet, muddy fields.

THE UNITED STATES

The heavy soil of the Midwest is so thick that old, wooden plows broke quickly. A man called John Deere invented a stronger plow in the 1830s, and his company still makes plows today.

RECORD BREAKERS

That many tractors made a LOT of noise!

MOST TRACTORS

The world record for the most tractors plowing together was set on June 25, 2006, when 2,141 tractors plowed at the same time!

The most **draft horses** pulling plows at the same time was set when 84 draft horses plowed a field in 2015.

GET YOUR LLAMA-DIPLOMA

Well done, farmhand! You made it through the training. If you've been paying attention, this test should be no prob-llama . . .

Questions

1. What are two other names for plowing?

2. How would tractors of the future know where to go?

3. What do disc plows have instead of blades?

4. What do seeds need in order to grow?

5. What animal can be used to plow paddy fields?

You made that look easy! Welcome to the Happy Valley Farm family!

CERTIFICATE
OF APPRECIATION

LLAMA-DIPLOMA

Farmer Llama

HAPPY VALLEY FARM

Download your llama-diploma!

1. Go to **www.factsurfer.com**

2. Enter "**Plows**" into the search box.

3. Click on the cover of this book to see the available download.

ASLEEP ON THE JOB

Phew! All that plowing has tired me out! I think I'll put my hooves up and let modern technology do all the work.

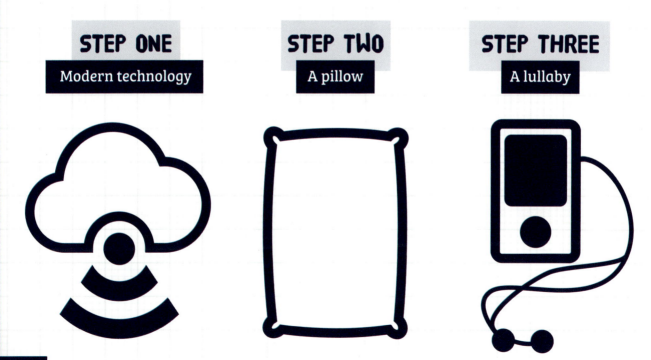

STEP ONE

Modern technology

STEP TWO

A pillow

STEP THREE

A lullaby

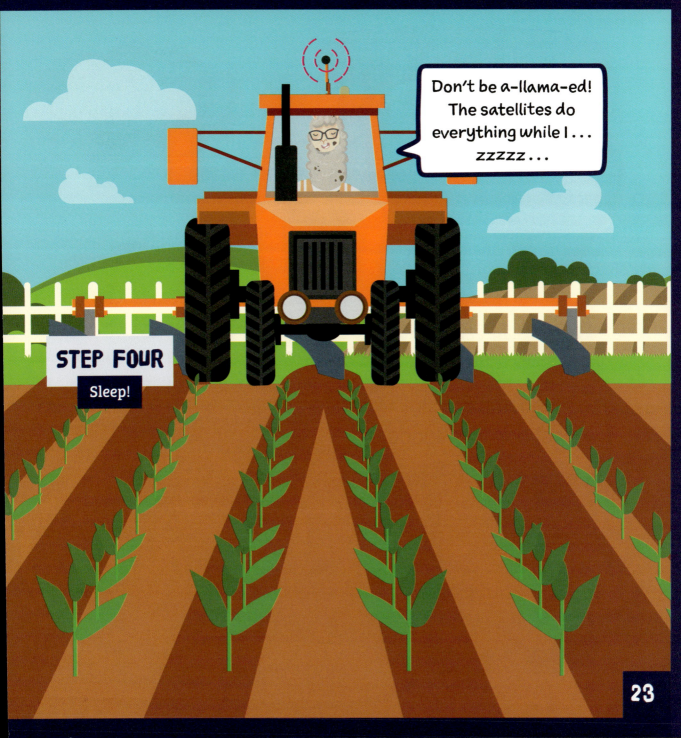

GLOSSARY

BLADES things with flat cutting edges, such as knives or saws

BURIES puts underground

CROPS plants that are grown on a large scale to be eaten or used

DEPTHS the distances from the top to the bottom of things

DISC a flat, thin, and circular object

DRAFT HORSES strong horses used to pull heavy objects

FARMHAND a person who works on a farm

SATELLITE a machine in space that travels around planets, takes photographs, and collects and sends information

WEEDS wild plants that are not wanted on farmland

INDEX

BUFFALO 9, 16

CHINA 16

COMPUTERS 10–11

CROPS 7, 16

DEERE, JOHN 17

HORSES 19

OXEN 9–10

SEEDS 5, 14–15

TRACTORS 6–7, 10–12, 18